CONTENTS

Words in **bold** are explained in the glossary on page 44.

NORWAY

Norway is one of the most northern countries of Europe. It is known for its beautiful and rugged (and cold!) environment. Norway is one of three Scandinavian countries, along with Denmark and Sweden. These Scandinavian countries have a shared history, as well as their own unique cultures and customs.

Svalbard

Nordkapp

Tromsø

Norway

Norwegian Sea

Bodø

Trondheim

Arctic Circle

Bergen

Stavanger

Oslo

Kristiansand

4

DK SUPER World

NORWAY

Discover the Scandinavian country of
Norway, with its majestic mountains,
stunning fjords and unique culture

PRODUCED FOR DK BY

Editorial Caroline Wakeman Literary Agency
Design Collaborate Agency
Graphic story illustrator Matt Garbutt

Project Editor Amanda Eisenthal
Senior Art Editor Gilda Pacitti
Managing Editor Carine Tracanelli
Managing Art Editor Sarah Corcoran
Production Editor Andy Hilliard
Production Controller Rebecca Parton
Publisher Sarah Forbes
Managing Director, Learning Hilary Fine

First published in Great Britain in 2025
by Dorling Kindersley Limited
20 Vauxhall Bridge Road,
London SW1V 2SA

The authorised representative in the EEA is
Dorling Kindersley Verlag GmbH. Arnulfstr.
124, 80636 Munich, Germany

Copyright © 2025 Dorling Kindersley Limited
A Penguin Random House Company
10 9 8 7 6 5 4 3 2 1
001–345885–Jun/2025

A CIP catalogue record for this book
is available from the British Library.
ISBN 978-0-2417-2669-3

Printed and bound in China

www.dk.com

This book was made with Forest
Stewardship Council™ certified
paper – one small step in DK's
commitment to a sustainable future.
**Learn more at www.dk.com/uk/
information/sustainability**

FASCINATING FACT!

The town of Nordkapp ("North Cape") in Norway is the most northern **inhabited** point in mainland Europe. Between mid-May and the end of July, the Sun doesn't set at all.

Nordkapp

Northern Lights Cathedral

Arctic Cathedral

Narvik Church

Lykkens Portal (Portal of Happiness)

Bryggen

Jotunheimen National Park

Akershus Fortress

Lindesnes Lighthouse

Bøkeskogen forest

ALL ABOUT NORWAY

Norges flagg

- 🏳 Flag: Norges flagg
- 📍 Capital city: Oslo
- 🧍 Population: Approx. 5.5 million
- 💬 Official languages: Norwegian, Sámi
- 💵 Currency: Kroner kr
- ✾ National flower: Purple heather
- 🐾 National animal: Elk (unofficially!)
- 🎵 National anthems: "Ja, vi elsker dette landet" ("Yes, we love this country"), "Sámi Soga Lávlla" ("The Song of the Sámi People")
- 👕 National dress: *Bunad, Gákti*
- ☆ Major export: Hydroelectric power, fishing, forestry

FIND OUT!

The capital city of Norway is Oslo, which means "meadow of the gods". Do you know what your country's capital city is? Can you find out what its name means?

Arctic and subarctic

Northern Norway is arctic, meaning it's inside the Arctic Circle. The rest is subarctic, just south of the Arctic Circle. In the north, the Sun doesn't ever set in summer (known as the midnight Sun) and doesn't ever rise in winter (known as the **polar** night).

Northern Lights

In the northern regions, on clear nights between September and April, you can see the Aurora Borealis, or Northern Lights. This is a colourful curtain of lights that swirl and flicker in the night sky. It is caused by electrically charged **particles** from the Sun interacting with **atmospheric gases**, producing a magical sky effect.

Svalbard

Svalbard is an **archipelago** about 933 kilometres (580 miles) north of Norway's mainland. It is actually closer to the North Pole than to the mainland of Norway. Just 2,500 people live in the main city of Longyearbyen, while at least 3,000 polar bears call Svalbard home!

FASCINATING FACT!

Svalbard is home to the Global Seed Vault: a secure underground vault that holds samples of more than a million seeds from across the world.

 **TERRAINS**

MOUNTAINS, FORESTS AND FJORDS

The land of Norway boasts rocky cliffs, thousands of islands, and many mountains, forests and fjords. There are large expanses of **tundra** in the north, as well as freezing forests that only exist in the subarctic regions of the world, just below the Arctic Circle.

Galdhøpiggen

Mountains

Most of Norway is mountainous. In fact, only 10 per cent of the land is flat enough for farming. The mountains are dotted with thousands of clear lakes, as well as stretches of **alpine tundra**. The tallest mountain is the Galdhøpiggen, at 2,469 metres (8,100 ft) high.

FASCINATING FACT!

The word tundra comes from a Sámi word meaning "barren land" or "treeless land".

Fjords

Norway's famous fjords are deep, narrow crevices in the land that lead out to sea. They are often filled with a mix of fresh water and, closer to the coast, sea water. Fjords have steep rugged sides and sometimes go so deep they can even have coral reefs at the bottom!

Coasts

Norway's long shape gives it miles and miles of coastline – about 28,953 kilometres (17,991 miles)! And that doesn't even include the coasts of the thousands of islands. The northern coast is surprisingly mild because the warmer waters of the **Gulf Stream** flow right past it.

Boreal forests

Boreal forests are only found in cold northern regions. The trees are hardy evergreens that can survive severe winters. They provide food and shelter for cold-weather animals like reindeer. They also absorb enormous amounts of carbon from the atmosphere, purifying the air.

SOGNEFJORDEN

Sognefjorden is the longest fjord in Norway, at 204 kilometres (127 miles) long. That's twice the distance from Earth to space! It's also the deepest fjord, at almost 1,308 metres (4,300 ft) deep. There are many beautiful villages along the edges of Sognefjorden.

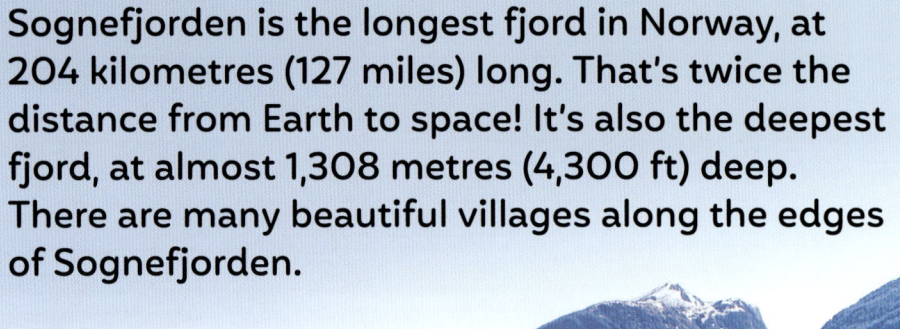

Waterfalls

Sognefjorden's walls are steep and during the summer you can see dozens of waterfalls cascading down the craggy cliffs. In the winter, these freeze into ice formations. At night, the waterfalls are said to be meeting places for trolls.

Formation of the fjord

During the last **ice age**, gigantic slow-moving **glaciers** carved deep valleys into the land. Once the glaciers reached the sea and melted away, salt water rushed in, eroding soft sandstone and forming the fjords.

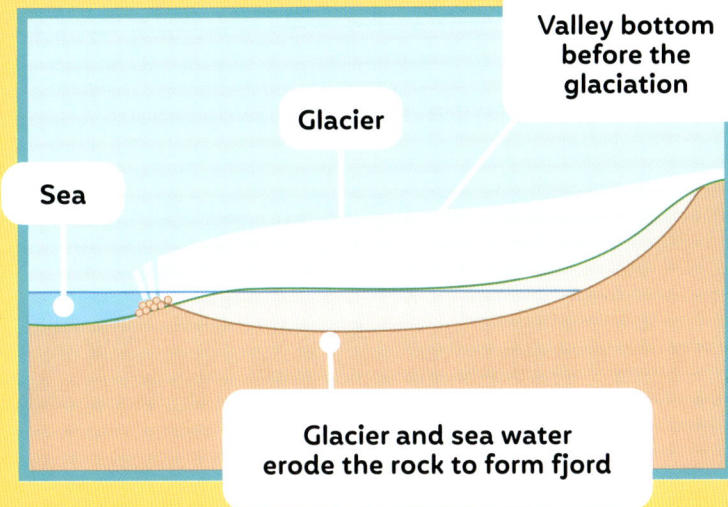

Valley bottom before the glaciation

Glacier

Sea

Glacier and sea water erode the rock to form fjord

Jostedalsbreen

North of the fjord is Jostedalsbreen, the largest glacier on mainland Europe. Melting water from the glacier feeds rivers that provide fresh water to nearby wildlife. This water also flows through **hydroelectric** power stations, providing **clean energy**.

Undredal

Picturesque towns

The towns along Sognefjorden are known for their beauty. The village of Flåm is home to the Flåmsbana train that runs through the valley of the fjord. Undredal is a tiny and beautiful village known for its goat cheese. Fjærland is a "book town", where every empty structure is turned into a bookshop or library.

FASCINATING FACT!

Jostedalsbreen is so big and cold, it affects the weather! It lowers the temperature of the air, turning moisture that would become rain into snow.

ARCTIC ANIMALS AND WINTER WILDLIFE

Animals and plants in Norway are particularly adapted to arctic and subarctic conditions. Unfortunately, global warming is transforming their natural habitats at a rapid rate, threatening their ways of living.

CREATURES OF THE COLD

Arctic fox

In winter, these little foxes have thick white fur that acts as camouflage. They hunt lemmings and other small mammals by listening for movements with their large ears and diving into the snow to snatch their prey with their paws. But they aren't fussy: Arctic foxes will eat berries, eggs, birds and even insects.

 **FASCINATING FACT!**

If there isn't enough food, Arctic foxes can slow their heart rate right down and sleep for up to two weeks, safe in their dens.

Lemming

These are small rodents that live in burrows underground. Every few years, Norwegian lemmings have a huge surge in population. To find enough food, they **migrate** in enormous groups, eating through any moss, grass, or other plant life in their way with their enormous teeth.

Rock ptarmigan

Ptarmigans (the p is silent) have white feathers in winter and rocky brown patterns on their feathers in summer. Their feet are feathered to help them walk in the snow on the tundra. The Svalbard **subspecies** of rock ptarmigan are bigger and heavier than their mainland cousins.

Reindeer

These antlered deer are incredibly well-adapted to their environments. Their two-toed hooves help them clamber over ice and scrape snow to find food. Dense blood vessels in their noses warm the air before it enters their bodies. Reindeer are the only mammals that can see ultraviolet light. This helps them to see in the long, dark winters.

COASTAL CREATURES

Norwegian Atlantic puffin
Puffins live mostly on the coasts and at sea. They hunt fish by diving into the water with their powerful wings. Their tongues have spines on them to stop their fishy prey wriggling out of their beaks. Puffins keep the same mate for their whole lives.

Norway lobster
These small **crustaceans** live in burrows in the soft sand of the seabed just off the coast. Their eyes are very sensitive to light, so if they live in shallow water, they only come out of their burrows at night. They are **omnivores** and will eat anything they can get their claws on!

Sea eagle
Also known as the white-tailed eagle, these are the largest birds of prey in Norway. From wingtip to wingtip, they measure almost 1.8 metres (6 ft). They build nests in coastal cliffs and mate for life. They hover low over the water and snatch out fish with their talons.

MARINE MAMMALS

Atlantic walrus

Walruses live in huge herds on the coasts of Svalbard and other Arctic islands. Their herds are usually separated into males and females. The males can grow tusks over 1 metre (3 ft) long! A layer of blubber up to 15 centimetres (6 in) thick keeps walruses warm in the freezing waters.

Narwhal

These whales have the fitting nickname, "unicorns of the sea". The males have an enormous horn that can grow up to 3 metres (10 ft) long. The horn also has 10 million nerve endings! Climate change and oil and gas development have put narwhals in the "vulnerable" status.

Ringed seal

These seals are so named because they have distinctive circle patterns on their pelts. They survive in the sea by making holes in the ice that they can breathe through. This allows them to avoid going within hunting distance of **predators** like polar bears or killer whales.

15

POLAR PLANTS

Norway spruce
These are evergreen trees, meaning they remain green and leafy all year round. They have long thin seed cones, can reach over 40 metres (130 ft) tall and can live for up to 1,000 years!

Kelp
Kelp forests grow underwater among shallow coastal rocks. Kelp forests are incredibly environmentally important. They are super-efficient at absorbing carbon dioxide and turning it into oxygen, and serve as protective homes for fish and molluscs, helping improve **biodiversity**.

Cloudberries
Cloudberries are also known as "Arctic gold". These goldish-orange bubbly berries are sought-after as delicious treats by animals and people alike! Birds and bears feast on the berries, while elks enjoy the woody stems. The berries thrive in the tundra and boreal forests of Norway.

THREATS

Climate change

The Arctic is warming at a rate three times faster than the rest of the world due to climate change. This threatens many of the species that rely on the ice and snow to survive, such as narwhals, polar bears, ringed seals, puffins and more.

Invaders

Pink salmon from the Pacific Ocean have invaded Norway's rivers and water systems. They can spawn in their thousands, competing for resources with local species and sometimes polluting rivers with their bodies when they die.

Hunting

Arctic foxes were prized for their bright white pelts, and were hunted almost to extinction in the early 1900s. Walruses, too, were over-hunted for their blubber (to use as oil), tusks (to make into ivory) and meat (for food). There are now bans on hunting both animals.

PEOPLE, LEGENDS AND PASTIMES

The Norwegian people are known for being community-focused, having a high standard of living and loving the outdoors! Norway has a rich culture that spans back thousands of years, before Viking times.

PEOPLE

Community

Norwegians are known for having a strong sense of community fairness. In fact, there is a Norwegian word *Janteloven* (the law of Jante) that is used to mean putting society before yourself. A focus on healthcare, welfare, education and equality mean that Norway is often regarded as one of the happiest countries in the world.

CUSTOMS

Gákti, Sámi national clothing

Sámi people

The Sámi are the **Indigenous** people of Norway. Their land of Sápmi inhabits parts of Norway, as well as Sweden, Russia and Finland. Historically, the Sámi are a culture of reindeer herders, fishers, hunters and gatherers. This way of life is still common for a lot of Sámi, though many also have less traditional jobs.

Sámi flag

Sámi culture

The Sámi have their own flag, simply called the "Sámi flag". They also have a traditional kind of song called a *yoik*. A *yoik* is not sung, it is *yoiked*. Someone might *yoik* a friend or a place they love, or to propose marriage. Reindeer herders sometimes *yoik* to ward predators away from their herds.

National clothing

The national dress of Norway is the *bunad*. The term applies to any clothes designed in the traditional Norwegian style. The Sámi traditional dress is the *gákti*. Both are worn on 17 May – Constitution Day. There is a lot of variety depending on where you come from.

LEGENDS

Gods and goddesses

Norse mythology tells of the gods and their home of Asgard. Odin is the leader. His son Thor is the god of war who creates thunder. The trickster god Loki is Odin's adopted brother. Frigg is the goddess of the sky and queen of Asgard. Their enemies are the *jötnar* giants.

Odin

Trolls

Folktales

Norwegian folktales are full of mythical creatures. Trolls are big human-like creatures, often slow and stupid, that live in forests and mountains. Elves are usually smart, beautiful and cruel, and love playing tricks on humans. The kraken is a giant tentacled sea monster, thought to be based on real-life giant squid seen by sailors.

Land of giants

Giants and trolls play a big role in Norway. The name of the national park Jotunheimen translates as "home of the giants". It is named for the *jötnar* – giants in Norwegian mythology. There's also a rock formation called Trolltunga ("troll's tongue") because it looks like a huge tongue sticking out from the cliff.

Trolltunga

PASTIMES

Right to roam

Norway has a law named *allemannsretten* ("everyman's right") that allows people access to any land that is not fenced off and is not used for gardens, farming or industrial purposes. People can hike and camp as they like, with a few rules: no littering, and stay at least 150 metres (about 500 ft) from anyone's house!

Dogsledding

Snow sports

Skiing is the national sport and a favourite pastime in Norway. It can even be done in summer on the mountains and glaciers. People also enjoy dogsledding, where they ride on a sled pulled across the snow by huskies. There are other cold-weather activities like cross-country skiing, snowboarding and ice hockey.

The concept of kos

The word *kos* refers to having a relaxing, comfortable time with simple pleasures. This might be having a nap in the Sun or enjoying a hot chocolate on a cold day. There are different words for *kos*. For example, *peiskos* means relaxing in front of a fire.

CHRISTIANITY AND SÁMI CULTURE

The main religion in Norway is Christianity. A large portion of the population are members of Christian churches, though a growing proportion claim to have no religion, too.

Church of Norway

Most Norwegians are members of the Christian Church of Norway. Christianity is the belief in a single God and the worship of God's son, Jesus Christ. Christians follow the teachings of Jesus, who promoted forgiveness and helping those in need.

Stave churches

These are medieval wooden churches carved with intricate patterns and figures. Stave churches are interesting because they are Christian churches that were built while some of the country was still **pagan**. This means they have pre-Christian pagan themes, such as dragons, Norse gods and pagan imagery, as well as Christian symbols.

Stave church

Sámi beliefs

The traditional Sámi belief system is based in animism: the belief that objects, places and animals have a spirit. The *noiade* is a Sámi shaman, who sometimes uses drums to go into a trance so they can communicate with spirits. Many Sámi today have embraced Christianity, sometimes alongside their traditional beliefs.

Drums

Sámi drums are made from wood and reindeer hide. The arrangement of symbols is unique to the drum's owner. They might be scenes of hunting or herding, or depictions of the owner's surroundings.

Sámi stories

Many Sámi stories describe how the world came to be and explain things like why animals look and behave the way they do. One tells of a fox running through the snow and sweeping his tail, sending glittering sparks drifting up into the sky and creating the Aurora Borealis. Some speak of the many gods, such as Horagállis (sometimes called Ukko), the god of thunder.

Other religions

About 3 per cent of people in Norway identify as Muslim. Communities from other cultures have also introduced other faiths such as Hinduism, Judaism, Buddhism and Sikhism.

SEASONAL CELEBRATIONS

Norway's holidays mostly take place when the days are longest, around May and June, and when they are shortest, in the depths of winter. While many of the holidays have Christian origins, they are generally celebrated by non-Christians too.

Constitution Day (Grunnlovsdagen)

Also known as National Day, 17 May celebrates the signing of the country's **constitution** after 400 years of Danish rule. People dress in the *bunad* and *gákti* traditional dress, wave flags and attend fairs.

Sámi National Day

Held on 6 January, this is the anniversary of the first international Sámi **congress**. Sámi culture is celebrated by flying the Sámi flag, using the Sámi language (which was once banned in certain places) and singing the Sámi anthem.

Christmas (Jul)

The main Christmas celebration in Norway takes place on 24 December. Presents are given and feasts are eaten. Christmas Day on the 25th and Saint Stephen's day on the 26th are also given as holidays.

Midsummer (Midsommar)

Midsummer is a festival that takes place on the longest day of the year, around 21 June. It is a mix of pagan rituals and Christian worship, as it coincides with the birth date of St John, celebrated as *sankthans*. Huge bonfires (*sankthansbålet*) are lit, and many have smaller bonfires with family and friends.

St Olaf's Day (Olsok)

On 29 July, Norwegians celebrate St Olaf, who is credited with bringing Christianity to Norway. In the village of Stiklestad, an outdoor theatre puts on a drama of St Olaf's life. The play has been performed every year since 1954!

Saint Lucy's Day (Santa Lucia)

This is a festival of lights in honour of the Christian saint, Saint Lucy, or Santa Lucia, on 13 December. Towns hold parades of young people dressed in white and carrying candles. One person is selected to represent Santa Lucia and wears a crown of candles at the head of the procession.

NORWEGIAN DELIGHTS

Norwegian cuisine tends to include a lot of fish, since Norway has a long coastline that gives people easy access to food from the sea. There are also many different techniques for preserving food, like pickling and **fermenting**, which stem from traditional methods of storing food for long winters.

Preserved fish

This winter specialty comes in many forms. *Sursild* is herring pickled with mustard seeds and spices in vinegar. *Rakfisk* is trout that's been fermented over several months. It is known for being extremely smelly!

Sursild

Brunost

This is a sweet, brown cheese. Different regions have their own recipes. Sometimes it is made with goat's milk, sometimes cow's milk and sometimes both. It can also be either hard enough to slice or soft enough to spread.

Smørbrød

This is an open sandwich, meaning there is no top slice of bread. Common toppings include cheese, sliced meat, smoked salmon, eggs and salad. For a big lunch, people might have a buffet of *smørbrød*.

Julebrus

This popular drink is served mostly around Christmas time. Its name translates as "Christmas fizz" and it comes in different fruity flavours.

Finnbiff

This is a traditional Sámi reindeer stew also known as *Reinskav*. The reindeer meat is frozen and then sliced thinly before cooking. It is made with mushrooms and cream.

Multekrem

This is a dessert of whipped cream sweetened with sugar and served with cloudberries. It is often served in *krumkake*: a kind of waffle cone.

Raspeballer

These are potato dumplings that go by many names depending what region you're in: *klubb, komler, komper, potetballer* and more. They are made of potato, stock and flour, and often served with meat or vegetables.

Eplemost

This is Norwegian apple juice. In winter, it is heated with herbs and spices for a warming treat.

RASPEBALLER

Raspeballer are boiled savoury dumplings, made with cooked potatoes and grated raw potatoes. This recipe makes about 12 dumplings.

MEAL IDEAS

Traditionally, *raspeballer* are served with:
- Buttered vegetables
- Cured or smoked meat
- Mashed swede
- Or even just butter and syrup!

Mashed swede

RASPEBALLER

Ingredients

- 500 g (1 lb) of raw potato
- 250 g (9 oz) of potatoes, peeled, cubed and cooked
- 80 g (2/3 cup) of barley flour (or wholewheat flour)
- 20 g (2 ½ tbsp.) of plain flour
- 1 tsp. of salt
- 1 litre (4 cups) of vegetable stock

Method

1. Peel the raw potatoes, then grate them (you can use a food processor or ricer). Try to squeeze as much of the water out of the raw potato as you can.
2. Take the cooked potatoes and mash them until they have no lumps.
3. Get a big bowl and mix together the mashed potatoes, raw potatoes and the flour and salt. Keep mixing until it forms a dough.
4. Make sure the mixture is cool, then form the dumpling balls! Dip a large spoon in water and use it to help you mould 12 balls, all the same size.
5. Put the stock into a large pot and turn it up high so it reaches a boil.
6. Once the stock is boiling, turn the heat down to medium and ask an adult to place the dumplings into the water using your spoon.
7. Let the dumplings simmer for 30-40 minutes. If the stock is still boiling, turn the heat down to a low-medium.
8. To check if the dumplings are done, take one dumpling out with a slotted spoon and slice it open. It will be hot, so be careful! If the dumpling has the same texture and colour all the way through, they are done.

ADULT SUPERVISION REQUIRED

LIVING AND WORKING

In Norway, most people live around the coastal edges because so much of the country is mountainous inland. More than 80 per cent of people live and work in the more southern regions, in urban areas around cities like Oslo and Bergen.

Norwegian houses

Houses in Norway have steep pointed roofs so the snow can't gather too heavily. They are often painted bright colours and made of wood because it is easy to insulate. More than half of homes have wood burners in case of power cuts.

FASCINATING FACT!

It's not unusual for there to be turf on the roof to help insulate homes for extra warmth!

Going to school

In Norway, pupils graduate from primary to lower secondary school in year 8 and can choose to leave school after year 10. However, many pupils stay on and go to upper secondary school for three more years. In all schools, Sámi children can choose to be taught in the Sámi language.

School stages

**Primary:
6–12 years old**

**Lower secondary:
13–16 years old**

**Upper secondary:
16–19 years old**

Major industries

Norway has a **public health system**, and more people are employed in the health sector than any other sector. **Renewable energy** is also a big industry, in particular solar power and **hydropower**. Norway is also a world leader in making electric ships!

Major exports

One of the main Norwegian exports is fish and seafood. They export around 1.5 million tonnes (1.7 million tons) of seafood a year! There is also a strong forestry industry that supplies wood and paper. Government policies make sure that forestry is **sustainable** by ensuring that trees are not cut down faster than they can regrow.

KAIA'S DAY

Name: Kaia Karlsen
Age: 10
Lives: Trondheim
Family: Mum and Dad

Hei! My name's Kaia, and this is my day in year 4.

It's December, so it's still dark outside when I wake up. I get dressed and go downstairs for my porridge (*havregrøt*). Today I have it with berries and cinnamon and a bit of jam.

I brush my teeth and pack my bag: pencil case with my coloured pencils, water bottle, workbooks and school tablet. My dad walks me to school and we meet Markus and Mads on the way – they're identical twins, but I can tell them apart.

Pappa
(Dad)

Me

Mamma
(Mum)

We play around in the playground until the bell rings at 8:30. Then we go in and take our coats and outdoor clothes off. We swap our snow boots for our indoor shoes and put everything in our lockers.

It's reading time first thing, so I pick a book – it's a comic book about dragons – and read until the teacher says reading time is over. Next, we have social studies. We do a worksheet about maps while our teacher tells us some interesting stuff. Did you know that sometimes mapmakers put in fake place names so that they can tell if someone copies their map?

We have a snack break and head out into the playground. It's nearly 10 o'clock so it's starting to get light. After break, we have art class using paints. I like my coloured pencils best, but I'm good with paints too. Mads is doing a dinosaur, so I paint a bigger dinosaur.

Before lunch, it's time to clear up. We put the paints away and tidy up the mats and wash our hands. We also put away our things and make sure the classroom is neat for the afternoon. Then it's lunch time!

We all get our packed lunches (*matpakker*) and go to the lunch hall. We usually have *brødskiver* in our lunches. Mads and Markus have smoked salmon and cheese. I have pâté and cucumber on one and prawns and mayonnaise on the other. I also have some brown cheese (*brunost*) slices and fruit.

Brødskiver: A kind of sandwich with just one slice of bread and various toppings.

Pålegg: Toppings for the *brødskiver.*

When we're done, we sort our recycling and then go outside to play tag with the rest of our class.

In the afternoon, we have science. We are learning about animal adaptations. That's when animals change over time to be better suited to their environments, like how polar bears have special fur with hollow hairs that trap in heat. Then we have an English lesson on our tablets.

We tidy up again and the end-of-school bell rings at 2pm. It's already starting to get a bit dark. Mads and Markus get picked up, but I go to SFO, where I usually see my friend Shaivya from year 5. She lives around the corner from me.

In SFO, we do things like reading, drawing, crafts and games. In the summer, we might go to the park or the beach. This week, I'm learning to knit a red scarf. After that, Shaivya and I build things with plastic bricks and play a board game.

SFO, or *skolefritidsordning:* After-school club.

My dad comes to get Shaivya and me at 5pm. For dinner, we're having fish soup (*fiskesuppe*), so I wash my hands and change and come down to eat. After dinner, I play in my room for a bit. I didn't get any homework today, but my mum and I are reading a book together, so after I put my pyjamas on we sit down and read a few chapters. That always makes me sleepy.

Good night (*god natt*)!

LAND AND INDEPENDENCE

People have inhabited Norway for 10,000 years. Historically, the Sámi people were hunters and trappers who followed the migration routes of the reindeer in the north. Norse communities further south were hunter-gatherers. Around 50 BCE, they became farming societies. At first, the two peoples lived independently of each other.

FASCINATING FACT!

The Vikings were warriors who spread across Europe to raid, loot and trade. They travelled as far as Canada in the west and Iraq in the east.

Vikings

Around 800 CE, the Viking era began. Vikings were Norse raiders and warriors, as well as traders and boatbuilders. They lived in family-centred communities led by chieftains. King Harald Fairhair united the various settlements into a single nation, beginning Norway as a country.

Paganism and Christianity

The Vikings were pagan, believing in the gods Odin, Thor, Frigg and more. At first, the pagans rejected Christianity, but it became common under King Olaf II in the 1020s. In 1066, the Viking King Harald Hardrada died in England, ending the Viking era and culture of raiding.

Losing land

In 1397, Norway formed a union with the Danish Queen Margaret I, beginning 400 years of Danish rule. Norwegians began colonising northern Sámi lands and enforcing country borders, interrupting the nomadic Sámi ways. In 1814, Denmark lost Norway to Sweden.

Independence and World Wars

In 1905, Norway finally became a fully independent country with its own **monarchy**. In 1913, women were given the right to vote. During World War II, Germany invaded Norway and occupied it until the German defeat in 1945.

Modern times

Today, Norway has a powerful economy thanks to natural resources like oil, gas and forests. It is a **democracy** with an elected government and prime minister. The monarchy no longer rules the country.

King Harald Fairhair statue

Nordic gods

Queen Margaret I

Oslo

ASKELADDEN AND THE TROLL

Askeladden's family were not well off.

One day, Askeladden and his two big brothers were sent out to bring back firewood to sell.

You can carry the wood sack, Aske-little!

But the woods were riddled with trolls.

I'll eat you all!

Askeladden's brothers fled in fear, but not Askeladden...

Askeladden took out his lunch: a lump of old hard cheese.

Oh yeah? Watch this. I can crush rocks with my bare hands!

He crumbled the cheese in his hand.

Hmmm. Okay, I can respect that. What do you want in my woods?

My family have no money. I've got to bring back firewood for us to sell.

Tell you what, boy, if you can beat me in an eating contest, I'll give you a heap of gold.

Deal!

The troll was much bigger than Askeladden. But trolls were not very clever, and Askeladden had a plan.

As they walked to the troll's cave, Askeladden stuffed his wood sack up his shirt.

Alright boy, porridge-eating contest!

Let's see what you've got!

Moving too quickly for the troll's slow eyes to see...

Askeladden filled the sack under his shirt as he pretended to eat.

The troll got fuller...

and fuller...

and fuller.

Stop! I can't take any more. You win, boy.

THE NORSE GODS OF ASGARD

The pagan Viking gods live in the heavenly realm of Asgard. Asgard connects to other realms by a bridge called the Bifrost. Read these descriptions of the Norse gods of Asgard.

Odin

The one-eyed king of the gods and the god of war, wisdom and magic is also known as the All-Father. Odin's companions are two ravens, Hugin and Mugin, and two wolves, Geri and Freki.

Frigg

Queen of Asgard and goddess of fertility and children, Frigg is brave and wise and has the power to see the future.

Thor

Thor is the son of Odin and god of thunder and war. He is strong, good and easily angered. He controls storms and protects humanity with his magic hammer, Mjöllnir.

Baldur

God of light and forgiveness, Baldur is Odin and Frigg's son. He is fair, beautiful and kind. He is immune to disease, and the only thing that can defeat him is... mistletoe!

Loki

This shapeshifting trickster god was actually born a *jötunn* (giant) but became the adopted brother of Odin. He loves to make plots and sow chaos, but he's also silly and playful.

Freya

Goddess of love and beauty, Freya is caring and gentle. She makes prophecies and rides a chariot pulled by two huge cats, Bygul and Trjegul.

How are the gods described?
angry, beautiful, brave, caring, fair, gentle, good, kind, playful, silly, strong, wise

What are they gods of?
beauty, children, family, fertility, forgiveness, light, love, thunder, tricks, war, wisdom

Special powers or items
cat, chariot-riding, controlling storms, hammer, immunity, magic, prophecies, raven, seeing the future, shapeshifting, wolf

Create your own Norse god or goddess. Give them a name and write a description using the vocabulary boxes to help you.

- What special abilities do they have?
- What special items do they use?
- What do they look like?
- What is their personality?

GLOSSARY

Agriculture The practice of farming.

Alpine tundra Cold areas at high elevation, such as on mountains, that have few trees and plants because the ground beneath the soil is permanently frozen.

Archipelago A group or chain of islands.

Atmospheric gases The gases in the Earth's atmosphere, such as oxygen, nitrogen, argon and carbon dioxide.

Biodiversity Variety in plant and animal life.

Boreal forest A forest that grows in northern regions where temperatures are below freezing for at least half the year.

Clean energy Energy that does not produce a lot of carbon dioxide.

Colonisation The act of taking control of a land and settling by force, often displacing people who already exist there.

Congress A formal political meeting.

Conservation The preservation and protection of animals, habitats and ecosystems.

Constitution A document that sets out the laws, beliefs and rules for a country.

Crustacean An aquatic creature without a spine that usually has a hard shell, such as a lobster or shrimp.

Democracy A form of government in which the people in power are elected by the general population.

Ecological Relating to the environment and ecosystems.

Ecosystem A community of plants, animals and other environmental factors that exist together with relationships and interactions that affect each other.

Elected government A government who was voted in by the people.

Fermented A chemical process applied to food and drinks that breaks down certain substances. It can be used to improve flavour and preserve food.

Glacier A huge mass of slow-moving ice.

Gulf Stream A stream of warm water that flows from the Gulf of Mexico.

Hydropower A form of renewable energy generated by water.

Ice age A long period of cold temperatures, in which glaciers cover much of the land.

Indigenous People whose ancestors were the earliest inhabitants of a land or those who inhabited a land before colonists arrived.

Inhabit To live in or occupy a particular place or area.

Invasive species A species that is non-native to an area but that has been introduced to and colonised that area. They are usually harmful to their environments.

Migrate Move from one place to another. For animals, this is usually done in groups and timed with seasons.

Mountain range A group or chain of mountains, usually with a name.

Norse Related to Scandinavia in the past, often the Viking era and before.

Omnivores Animals that eat both meat and vegetation.

Pagan Religious belief in nature and a set of multiple gods. Historically, this was often used to mean non-Christian.

Particle A tiny fragment, such as a molecule.

Polar Relating to regions around the North or South Pole.

Predator An animal that hunts and preys on other animals.

Public health system Healthcare that is available to everyone for free or for small fees.

Renewable energy Energy from a natural source that won't run out. This includes solar power, hydropower and wind power.

Standard of living How comfortably people can live. It is measured by wealth and access to things like education, electricity, clean water and suitable housing.

Subspecies A branch of a main species that is slightly different to the main species. For example, tiger is a species, and Bengal tiger is a subspecies.

Sustainable Affects an environment in such a way that the natural areas and resources can exist in future generations.

Tundra Cold areas with few trees and plants because the ground beneath the soil is permanently frozen.

Urban Related to towns or cities.

INDEX

ACKNOWLEDGMENTS

The publisher would like to thank the following for their kind permission to reproduce their photographs:

(Key: a-above; b-below/bottom; c-centre; f-far; l-left; r-right; t-top)

Adobe Stock: Kushnirov Avraham 22, Sergey Bogomyako 9tr, marysckin 27clb, Lin V 24t, william87 37br; **Alamy Stock Photo:** James Berry 37tr, Chronicle 42tr, NTB 25cl, World History Archive 37cr; **Dreamstime.com:** Ab2147272 27tl, Ernest Akayeu 20tr, 28-29b (vegetables), 42-43 (Norse gods), F Baarssen 9cl, Natalia Chernyshova 7clb, Dmitry Chulov 11cla, Everst 21t, Frank Fichtmueller 13tl, Peter Hermes Furian 4cl, 4b, Boris Gavran 8, Aleksei Gorodenkov 31tl, Menno Van Der Haven 36, Jiri Hera 29bc, Andrei Hrabun 25bl, Oleksandra Klestova 33bc, Tetiana Kozachok 32-33 (Stationery), Dalia Kvedaraite 14b, Tomas Marek 11clb, Merfin 31ca, Igor Mojzes 21bl, Alexander Mychko 27cla, Nanisimova 10, Oksanabratanova 27bl, Roxxanna1 16tl, Vladimir Seliverstov 17tl, Shaiith 26t, Alexander Shalamov 21cl, Shapicingvar 6, Natalia Sokko 16cl, Oleksandr Sutchenko 31crb (x3), Adrian Szatewicz 9br, Stefano Zaccaria 30; **Getty Images:** The Image Bank Unreleased / Michel Setboun 23t; **Shutterstock.com:** Shpadaruk Aleksei 35r, Valda Butterworth 14tr, dreakrawi 19t, Ron Ellis 10b, everst 18, Andrey_Fokin 30b, Petros Goulas 25tl, GrumJum 28crb, Jan_Kuchar_Photo 16bl, Lyudmyla Kharlamova 28-29 (paper), 32tr, Lauritta 24b, lazydog20 7cl, Roland Magnusson 19cl, Borodacheva Marina 32-33 (Background), 34-35 (Background), Joe McDonald 15tl, Elizaveta Melentyeva 5, Muhammadphotoes 15cl, Hisa_Nishiya 32b, Konstantin Novikov 17tr, Nsit 28tr, Maciej Olszewski 14tl, Sofiia Popovych 34cb, Pro Symbols 26br, railway fx 6l, Risto Raunio 17b, Pavlo S 4br, See U in History 37cra, Simon's passion 4 Travel 23cl, SofieLion 12, Bjorn H Stuedal 13tr, Surajkalangada 26bl, David Pineda Svenske 20cl, Frederik Tellerup 19bl, Thx4Stock team 31clb (x2), TRphotos 7t, Tupungato 20br, urfin 29bl (cl), Sergey Uryadnikov 15bl, V. Belov 37crb, v.iraa 34-35 (Stickers), Karen Yomalli 13b

Cover images: *front:* **Getty Images:** Mike Hill br; **Getty Images / iStock:** lightpix cr, Nirut Punshiri t/ (Background); **Shutterstock.com:** *alaver bl; Back:* **Adobe Stock:** *Sergey Bogomyako tl, william87 bl;* **Shutterstock.com:** *SofieLion cl*

All of the books in the *Super World* series have been reviewed by authenticity readers of the cultures represented to make sure they are culturally accurate.